19.99

StoryBuilding

StoryBuilding

100+ Ideas for Developing Story & Narrative Skills

Sue Jennings

First published in 2010 by
Hinton House Publishers Ltd
Newman House, 4 High Street, Buckingham MK18 1NT, UK
T +44 (0)1280 822557   F +44 (0) 560 3135274   E info@hintonpublishers.co.uk

www.hintonpublishers.co.uk

© 2010 Sue Jennings

Worksheet illustrations 1–5 by Suzanne Hall
Worksheet illustration 6 by Chloe Gerhardt

All rights reserved. The whole of this work including texts and illustrations is protected by copyright. No part of it may be copied, altered, adapted or otherwise exploited in any way without express prior permission, except in accordance with the provisions of the Copyright, Designs and Patents Act 1988 or in order to photocopy or make duplicating masters of those pages so indicated, without alteration and including copyright notices, for the express purpose on instruction and examination. No parts of this work may otherwise be loaded, stored, manipulated, reproduced, or transmitted in any form or by any means, electronic or mechanical, including photocopying or storing it in any information, storage or retrieval system, without prior written permission from the publisher, on behalf of the copyright owner.

British Library Cataloguing in Publication Data

A catalogue record for this book is available from the British Library.

ISBN-13: 978-1-906531-32-4

Printed and bound in the United Kingdom

*To Sarah Watts
who has helped
with so many stories.*

Contents

About the Author	xi
Acknowledgements	xi

INTRODUCTION — 1
Aims — 1
Storytelling Traditions — 1
Soaps, Shakespeare & Shamans — 3
Storytelling in Everyday Life — 6

DEVELOPING STORYTELLING SKILLS — 9
Why Stories? — 9
Storytelling & Child Development — 10
How StoryBuilding Works — 11
Why Storytelling? — 15

SECTION 1 TO BEGIN AT THE BEGINNING: THE STORY STARTERS

1 STARTING WITH PLACE: 'WHERE?' — 19
Preliminary Work — 21
Ideas for Discussion 1 — 22
Homework Suggestions — 23
Ideas for Discussion 2 — 24
Story Starters — 25
Ideas for Discussion 3 — 28

2 STARTING WITH EVENTS: 'WHAT HAPPENED?' — 29
Preliminary Work — 30
Ideas for Discussion 1 — 31
Homework Suggestions — 32

Ideas for Discussion 2	33
Story Starters	34
Ideas for Discussion 3	37

3 STARTING WITH CHARACTERS: 'WHO?' — 39

Preliminary Work	40
Ideas for Discussion 1	41
Homework Suggestions	42
Ideas for Discussion 2	43
Story Starters	44
Ideas for Discussion 3	47

4 STARTING WITH 'WHAT ELSE?' — 49

Developing Characters	49
Preliminary Work	49
The Story of the Old Woman	49
Ideas for Discussion 1	51
Homework Suggestions	52
Ideas for Discussion 2	53
The Story of Fred	54
Ideas for Discussion 3	56
Homework Suggestions	57
Ideas for Discussion 4	58

- **Developing the Atmosphere** — 59
Preliminary Work	59
Ideas for Discussion 1	60
Homework Suggestions	62
Story Starters	63
Ideas for Discussion 2	65

- **Developing the Props** — 67
Preliminary Work	67
Ideas for Discussion	68
Story Starters	69

- Developing Places & Spaces — 71
  - Preliminary Work — 71
  - Ideas for Discussion 1 — 72
  - Story Starters — 74

5 STARTING WITH TIME: 'WHEN?' — 77

- Preliminary Work — 79
- Ideas for Discussion 1 — 81
- Homework Suggestions — 82
- Story Starters — 83
- Ideas for Discussion 2 — 85
- Story Starters — 86
- Ideas for Discussion 3 — 89
- Developing the Concept of Time — 89
- Ideas for Discussion — 90

6 DEVELOPING THE PLOT & STORY ENDINGS — 91

- Ideas for Discussion 1 — 93
- Homework Suggestions — 94
- Ideas for Plot Development — 95
- Ideas for Story Endings — 99

SECTION 2 RESOURCES

Story Starter Worksheets — 103

References — 109

Further Reading — 111

About the Author

Sue Jennings PhD is a storyteller, play and dramatherapist and trainer. She has extensive experience working with children and teenagers of all ages both in schools and the community. She travels to Malaysia, Israel, Romania and India to develop her work on StoryBuilding, especially with groups with PDD, and those with behavioural and emotional difficulties. She has published extensively (www.suejennings.com), and her PhD thesis is also a book about the Temiar people of Malaysia.

Sue, with her husband Peter, is director of The Rowan Centre, Glastonbury, providing training and workshops for parents and volunteers, as well as teachers, clinicians, arts workers and therapists. She promotes StoryBuilding in local schools, nurseries and care homes. Sue is also Project Leader of UK charity The Rowan Tree Trust.

Acknowledgements

To all my storyteller friends, and special thanks to Sue Hall for her patient production assistance.

Introduction

Aims

The primary aim of this book is to make storytelling available for everyone, especially children and young people. It will help to provide basic storytelling skills for teachers, parents and care-workers to enable them to encourage storytelling in others. As storytelling is traditionally an oral skill, rather than a written one, it can reach a range of children and young people, especially those who struggle with literacy and the written word.

Reading and writing skills are difficult for many, and the development of the oral skills needed for creating and communicating a story can help to develop and build literacy skills. Developmentally, a baby communicates first through sounds, and then words and then finally learns to read and write. However, we do not need reading and writing skills in order to tell a story, spin a yarn or weave a tale.

Storytelling Traditions

Traditionally, every culture had its own form of stories, storytelling and storyteller: folk tales, epic stories, creation myths; stories of history, stories for healing, stories for telling the future; bards, shaman and soothsayers.

Many stories were accompanied by music or were told in the form of chants or songs. Storytellers were believed to be inspired by the Divine or were a mouth piece for the gods. Often they underwent a lengthy period of training or apprenticeship. In modern times many of these traditions have been lost or superseded by technology. There has been a shift away from neighbourhood or village communities and storytelling is no longer a means of creating social cohesiveness.

Nevertheless, there are many groups such as the UK-based Society for Storytellers who are reviving the art of storytelling and supporting schools and other groups in continuing the oral tradition rather than focussing on the written word alone.

> The old village men in Kyrgyzstan say that to be a true Manas storyteller, one needed a long apprenticeship and then a panel of judges would decide whether you were good enough to carry the tradition forward. The Manas epic is some 500,000 words in length which is longer than the *Mahabharata* or the *Odyssey* and *Iliad* put together.

> The Temiars of Malaysia are very strict about when storytelling is permitted. It has to be when there is no singing or dancing; there is no musical accompaniment and it is a male activity. Their stories are usually creation myths or specific tales of events that ensued when any Temiar broke the main rules of their society.

In this book we will draw on some of the inspirations for great stories and traditions, but its main purpose will be to make the art of creating and telling stories accessible to children and young people, and to show them the joy of storytelling, especially those who have special educational needs. Storytelling often requires reflection and children and young people can become disengaged if they feel they must be creative on the spot. Many fear ridicule, especially if they have communication or learning difficulties.

Soaps, Shakespeare & Shamans

Soap operas, whether on radio or television, introduce the basic idea of a narrative which is a technique we can develop in our storytelling.

In the UK in the 1950s, a radio soap 'The Archers' told the continuing story of a rural community and aimed to impart information to avid listeners, and is still going after more than 55 years. Another soap about a suburban doctor's family only lasted for 21 years; it ended when listeners stopped identifying with the characters.

The cancelling of some soaps and the longevity of others shows that the power of stories lies in the ease with which the audience can identify with them. Characters are chosen because they represent a type rather than an individual: a feisty granny, an aggressive teenager, a harassed mum and so on. The language used is easily understood by the greatest number of viewers or listeners, and plots revolve around situations that seem familiar.

Often fan mail, advice or criticism is addressed to a character in a soap rather than the actor – the plot line reaches people in their own lives. People feel that someone knows how they feel. Script writers also try to ensure that plot lines include social information regarding people with learning difficulties, homosexuality, abortion, racism, medical facts and many other themes that may educate and inform people.

It may be that the stories of the soaps have, to a great extent, replaced the social function of community and spiritual leaders.

It could be asked whether there is much difference between the shaman in a trance whose performance to a captive audience includes admonition of certain types of behaviour, and information about where to hunt and the storylines of soaps that address similar behavioural themes and are also addressed to a captive audience, although of a far greater number of people.

The big difference of course is that that the shaman gives a live performance, in comparison to a radio or television. However, live performances of social and historical stories by storytellers, community workers, actors, politicians and clerics do make a difference to the activity of storytelling. These live stories are personalised for the people listening and can vary in time, content and rhythm. And, more often than not, it is live storytelling without a script that holds our attention. Traditional storytellers would travel from place to place and take the news with them; they would tell stories and accompany themselves with a tabor or flute: music and storytelling often go together in the traditional contexts.

Please don't dismiss the stories that children and young people learn from the television, as these may be their first contact with storytelling. These stories can be elaborated on and developed during your classes, but they are a good familiar starting point. Many children will have watched television stories from a young age and be familiar with a story structure even if they are not used to telling stories. So be prepared to watch a range of programmes and see for yourself how several different stories are woven into the whole drama; who is a part of whose story?

Another rich source of storytelling is the world of Shakespeare. Stories from Shakespeare can be seen as Elizabethan soap operas, full of jealousy, thwarted love, murder, rage, incest, rivalry and so on. Not really so very different from the contents of popular soap operas. Actor Ben Crystal (2008) gives us some wonderful insights into the similarities between Shakespeare and modern soaps, and describes how they share the same quality of piling event upon event, always ending a scene with a cliff-hanger. He goes on to say:

> If writers portrayed life as it really was, with all its silences and normal events – like the TV show *Big Brother Live* – we'd die of boredom (or exhaustion). Moreover, if we daily experienced what the characters in *East Enders* go through, the LAST thing we'd want to do is watch someone go through exactly the same thing.

There are many good stories by Shakespeare that reluctant pupils can discover through the medium of film, which could encourage further exploration, especially the modern version of *Romeo and Juliet* staring Leonardo DiCaprio, for example.

Storytelling in Everyday Life

Every time we meet a neighbour or wait at a bus stop or are delayed at the doctor's surgery, there is an exchange of stories. We create narratives about our lives, our children, our work and will vary the story depending on our audience. For example, we will tell the story of a car accident to our best friend in a very different way from how we might tell it to a parent. We might leave out things that some people may not approve of, or exaggerate something to improve our self-esteem. Essentially, we tell truth-based stories about events in our own lives.

If we look at any group of people or any culture anywhere in the world, it is clear that storytelling is a part of people's lives, and always has been. Stories are told for many reasons, and we even accuse people of 'making up a story' when a tale seems unbelievable. A commonly heard phrase when being told of a particularly complicated event, is 'If that was on television you wouldn't believe it!'

However, despite our watching of soap operas or listening to audio books or even seeing a traditional storyteller, the problem for many people is that they do not have the confidence to tell stories themselves. They do not see their dramatic rendition of what happened on holiday as a story.

Parents will buy their children a tape or CD of a story rather then read it themselves, because the actors 'do it better' and they have no confidence in telling or reading a story themselves. Many actors supplement their incomes by recording stories for radio or as audio books as well as making special recordings for people with visual impairments. It is now a selling point for a new children's book that it has an accompanying CD, with the story being read by a famous actor!

Developing Storytelling Skills

Why Stories?

Why should we tell stories to our children, students or others in our care? And why should we encourage children and young people to tell and create stories? What could be gained? The following are just some of the reasons that storytelling is important but there are many, many more.

- *Storytelling can increase self-esteem and confidence.*

- *Storytelling can improve communication skills.*

- *Storytelling can increase memory retention: children will remember an event if a story is created about it.*

- *Storytelling helps to develop the imagination.*

- *Storytelling stimulates all areas of learning.*

- *Storytelling can frame difficult experiences and make sense of them.*

- *Stories are the basis of forming a relationship with someone – in telling a story people are sharing something of themselves.*

This book will show how these issues can be addressed, along with plenty of ideas and storytelling techniques to develop them. The technique of 'StoryBuilding' is used, through which a story is built up, one stage at a time.

The following sections guide the reader through the basic stages of StoryBuilding. The approach has been developed with many different groups in many cultures and has enabled hundreds of children and young people to tell their own stories and to derive enormous pride and self-esteem from doing so.

Storytelling & Child Development

If young people have had a stimulating start to life, with plenty of 'live' stories, rhymes and songs they will already have an understanding of a story structure. From the age of around three years children will talk to themselves in story form with long monologues about make-believe. They will constantly ask 'What?', 'Where?' and 'Who?' questions. Three-year-olds listen intently to stories, and ask for their favourite one to be repeated over and over again. They have some idea of the present and the past, and understand the idea of waiting for something. By four years of age a child is able to tell long stories as well as listen to them, and reality and fantasy are often muddled up. They have added questions of 'Why?', 'When?' and 'How?' which are frequently asked, and they are interested in the meaning of words. By the age of five children delight in storytelling and acting out stories on their own or with other children. They also enjoy speaking or singing rhymes as well as jokes and riddles.

However, not all children will have had such stimulating and secure beginnings in life and many will need to catch up on developmental stages. This is where StoryBuilding can help a child to understand the place and the event, the people, props and atmosphere, the plot and the time-frame in which stories take place. We will use each of these stages in our ideas for storytelling.

The '5 W's + H' (Where, What, Who, Why, When, + How?) are addressed sequentially in this book with Story Starter ideas for each question.

How StoryBuilding Works

StoryBuilding starts with simple beginning phrases about the 'Where?' of the story, where does the action take place? We will then explore the 'What?' of the story; what is the event that is happening? Then the 'Who?' of the story is explored; who is the main character in this story or perhaps there are several people. These introductions are then elaborated at many levels using 'What else?', describing the atmosphere, feelings and props; what else is in the sequence to hold the reader's or listener's attention?

We will move on to the 'When?' of the story and the introduction of the concept of time; when exactly did the event take place (very important to a detective, for instance), and how distant was it in the past or is it happening well into the future, like in many science-fiction stories. This leads to the 'How?' of the story which is the construction of a plot, and how to lead into what actually happens. Finally, different endings and means of closing our stories are described.

Throughout, different types of storytelling are considered, including the personal, the social and the creative.

Photocopiable story sheets are provided for completion, which will enable children and young people to experience the achievement of creating a story.

However, the main aim of this book is to provide ideas for starting stories, what follows is a lot easier! If a reader is not engaged by the opening phrases of a story they will often not read on, and if a storyteller does not hold us with their opening lines we will probably stop listening.

Getting started

Initially, I suggest that you abandon the use of paper and pens, and focus on discussion and suggestions from the group. Try working with children or young people in a circle, using a large white board or sheet of paper for writing down contributions from the group and aim to establish an inclusive strategy. It is not a question of accepting what you feel are the best ideas, this is an approach where everyone's ideas are important. There is no one right way to create and tell a story.

Ground rules

It is important to establish the ground rules of no gratuitous violence and no inappropriate sexual references. Mild swearing can probably be allowed if it is appropriate to a character in a story. It can also be unhelpful, depending on your group, if wrongdoers end up 'getting away with it' and law-abiders suffer losses. Try to keep in mind that one reason for telling stories is to help people to understand the implications of their actions.

Equipment

If it seems that the group need to be 'doing' then have to hand extra card, paper, board and marker pens. The group may want to create pictures and illustrations or write down odd words or ideas. However, these should be ideas suggested to the group rather than tasks they are obliged to do.

As mentioned above, storytelling is largely an oral activity and there is little need for elaborate equipment. The white board and coloured markers are really all you need; as work progresses you can use card and coloured pens, extra white boards, newspapers and magazines, scissors and glue.

As the group's skills develop and confidence builds, people can move on to writing down their own stories and working in smaller groups or on their own.

You can also develop ideas for storytelling using puppets or story baskets or bags. Additional props such as postcards, fridge magnets and snow globes also have their place in a storytelling setting. However, above all it is important to keep things as simple as possible; it is easy for storytelling to become cluttered and an excess of props can sometimes get in the way of the story.

Why Storytelling?

Storytelling

* *Can increase self-esteem and confidence: the sheer achievement of creating a story will help children and young people feel better about themselves.*

* *Improves communication skills; gradually children will find they can tell stories, increase vocabulary and develop variations in their tone of voice.*

* *Can increase memory retention; children will remember an event if told a story about it.*

* *Helps to develop the imagination and confidence, these ideas will help to stimulate the child's imagination and increase their confidence in contributing to class discussion.*

* *Stimulates all areas of learning; these structures can be used for storytelling in any subject area.*

* *Can frame difficult experiences and make sense of them. Many children and young people have confusing experiences; storytelling enables them to make sense of parallel stories which can throw light on their own situation.*

* *Is the basis of forming a relationship with someone. When telling stories people are sharing something of themselves. Most stories involve interaction with others and children and young people can learn appropriate ways of relating to others.*

Section One

To Begin at the Beginning: The Story Starters

1 Starting with Location: 'Where?'

Many stories locate the events in a specific space, while others have a more general idea of place. For example the story may start: 'In the house at the end of Benedict Street…' or 'In a faraway land…'

Children and young people often feel insecure if they do not know where something is going to happen. For example, are all my classes in the same room or will some be held somewhere else?

Some children can feel 'frozen in space', they become disorientated because they do not where they are. This can happen if they are suddenly removed from their home space if they are taken into care and then placed into another home and maybe another. Parents can make sudden house moves because of financial difficulties, new job opportunities or a grandparent coming to live. Teenagers can lose their precious bedroom space because they are made to share with step-brothers or sisters, or there is a flood or fire in the home, or even if they are sent to boarding school.

Knowing where we are is very important for feelings of security and safety, and it gives us a secure base. By starting our stories with a clear idea of place and space we can also 'anchor' the experiences of the children and young people. The following are a range of 'place and space starters' from adult stories:

'The old Spanish house sat back away from the street, nestled behind lush tropical foliage and towering palms.'
Plea of Insanity by Jillian Hoffman

'Water splashing. A gray mosaic tile tub sunk deep into the terra-cotta floor. Water pours slowly from an old brass spout, and darkness pours through the window.'
Book of the Dead by Patricia Cornwall

'If you shall chance, Camillo, to visit Bohemia on the like occasion whereon my services are now on foot, you shall see, as I have said, great difference betwixt our Bohemia and your Sicilia.'
The Winter's Tale by William Shakespeare

'My earliest memory is of sitting in front of the nursery fireguard in the evening…'
Memories by Lucy Boston

Perhaps the longest place starter I have discovered in a story for young people is the beginning of *The Amber Spy Glass*, the third volume in Philip Pullman's trilogy *His Dark Materials*:

'In a valley shaded by rhododendrons, close to the snow line, where a stream milky with melt-water splashed and where doves and linnets flew amongst the immense pines, lay a cave, half hidden by the crag above and the stiff heavy leaves that clustered below.'

In fact, the whole of the first page and a third of the second page are devoted to a description of place before there is any introduction of either people or plot.

Preliminary Work

Before starting to work on stories as a group, begin with some general discussion to start ideas flowing.

Start with a group discussion of space and stories: How important is the place where a story happens; does it matter where the story takes place? Discuss the places in which stories have happened – unusual spaces as well as conventional ones. You could also make use of some posters and pictures and discuss the sort of events that could have happened at these places. Keep this simple to start with, and identify the place and discuss where it is, before thinking of an event. For example:

- *Travel poster showing sea and sandy beach.*
- *Picture of an old castle.*
- *A postcard of a thatched cottage and garden.*
- *Travel poster of snow-covered mountains.*
- *Photograph of a factory complex.*
- *Brochure about a new hospital.*
- *Newspaper cutting of a railway station.*

> **Project Idea**
>
> The group could start a folder of pictures of places where things happen or where they might happen. Ask people to bring in pictures from advertisements, newspapers, magazines, postcards or photographs.

Ideas for Discussion 1

- *What is the most boring location for a story?*
- *Think of a silly place for a story to take place.*
- *What would be a really scary place for a story?*
- *Where would be an unusual place for a story?*
- *Could there be a shocking place for a story?*
- *Think of a secret or mysterious place for a story.*
- *What is an ordinary location for a story?*

Homework Suggestions

a) *In your favourite TV programme, how important are the locations where the action happens?*

b) *Watch a news programme and note how places are shown.*

c) *If you are planning to meet someone, are you specific or general about the meeting place?*

d) *Bring in junk mail or brochures that have pictures of interesting places.*

e) *Look at any story in a magazine or comic and see whether it begins with a description of a place.*

f) *Look for any leaflets or brochures that show different maps.*

g) *Look at all the front doors in your street: in what ways are they different? Materials? Colours? Neatness?*

Ideas for Discussion 2

- *Think of your favourite places to relax; to go on holiday; to meet friends; to have a picnic or party; to go walking*
- *Which place do the group not like to visit and why?*
- *Where do parents or other relatives like to go?*
- *Do you like to go with them?*

Story Starters

Now ask the group to start some basic stories based on places and what happens in them. These starters can be used for class discussion or small group work. Give everyone a sentence each and ask them to decide what comes next. Ask them to note how specific the references to places are and whether this makes a difference to the stories they come up with:

1	'In the market place…'
2	'In the house in Benedict Street…'
3	'On the bench in Malory Park…'
4	'In a faraway land…'
5	'In the middle of nowhere…'
6	'Across the valley…'
7	'In the kitchen in my house…'

Can we add just a few words to make these places more specific and give them more life? For example:

1a 'In the dusty market in old Baghdad…'

2a 'In the oldest house on St Benedict Street…'

3a 'On the new park bench in Malory Park…'

4a 'In a faraway land, on a river bank…'

5a 'In the middle of nowhere, there was a garage…'

6a 'Across the Welsh valley…'

7a 'On the table in my kitchen…'

A little more detail helps to extend these ideas:

8	'There were palm trees, a blue sky and the gentle lapping of the water…
9	'It was desolate, not a tree or house in sight…
10	'The forest was dense with creepers trailing between the trees…

Ideas for Discussion 3

✻ *When you enter a space or a new place, what is the first thing you notice? Some people notice machines or mechanical objects, others notice people and others notice things that are growing.*

✻ *Think about a place you have visited, what is the first thing you remember?*

2 Starting with Events: 'What Happened?'

Having established the ideas of spaces and locations where stories can happen, now move forward to an exploration of events that can happen in stories, what is happening at the beginning of a story?

Some stories begin with a description of an event. News reports frequently announce an event and then go on to tell us more; for example, 'There has been a serious explosion…' or 'A riot has taken place in…'

The event is often what hooks the audience and draws them into the story, and some events interest us more than others. Many events are very dramatic and some newspapers specialise in dramatising events to their full potential. Often, our first thought is 'What happened next?' and events of all sorts can then lead us into storytelling. The following are some examples of 'event starters' in books:

> 'I had seen the collision coming, but when it happened the impact was so abrupt and stunning that it shocked the sense out of me…'
> *An Indian Summer* by James Cameron

> 'The rumour spread through the city like wildfire…'
> *The Truth* by Terry Pratchett

> 'On the way out from the central desert we had an unexpected encounter which, brief as it was, had important consequences for me.'
> *The Heart of the Hunter* by Laurens Van Der Post

Preliminary Work

What do we mean by an event? An event can be described as something that happens. Some events are planned, such as a concert or sports fixture, others happen without warning such as accidents or train crashes. Develop a discussion about events that the group find interesting or boring. What sort of events do we watch on TV? Football matches? Concerts? The Olympics? Famous funerals? Famous weddings? These events can be used for starting stories. Make use of pictures or flyers as a visual stimulus for an event, such as:

* *Poster advertising a sale of carpets or books.*
* *Charity leaflet for a fund-raising concert.*
* *Postcard of a procession from another country.*
* *Announcement of a meeting to discuss a new road.*
* *Grand opening of a new stadium.*
* *Advertisement for a new film about aliens.*
* *Picture of a famous wedding.*

Project Idea

Encourage the group to create a second folder and bring in pictures and announcements of events, for example, theatre programmes, notices of grand openings, newspaper cuttings, pictures from magazines.

Ideas for Discussion 1

* *What do you notice first about a poster?*

* *What makes an event look interesting in a picture?*

* *Does a picture on a poster encourage you to go to an event?*

* *How do you feel about fund-raising events for charity?*

* *Do film posters make you want to know more about what happens?*

* *How would you feel if your picture was in a newspaper? What sort of event might be photographed?*

* *Can a picture tell us everything we need to know about an event or are words needed too?*

Homework Suggestions

a) *Bring in a picture of an event you would like to go to, and describe why it is important to you.*

b) *Bring in a picture of an event you would not like to attend. Would it be scary? Or boring?*

c) *Find an announcement or picture of an event that is unknown to you and guess what it could be about.*

d) *Find an announcement about an event that would really change your life. How might it do this?*

e) *Watch a report of an event on TV and think about what held your attention.*

f) *Find a programme or flyer from an event that someone else has attended. What can you understand from the programme? Would you want to go too?*

g) *Find a picture of something you think would be a very boring event. What would make it boring? The subject perhaps, or the place it is happening?*

Ideas for Discussion 2

- *What might make an event boring?*
- *Why would you go to one political meeting and not another?*
- *Do you have to go to events that older people arrange for you?*
- *If you could choose a special event to attend, what would it be?*
- *What sort of events do your parents go to?*
- *Have you ever wished you could go with your parents?*

Story Starters

Consider the following starters describing events and continue the sentences either in small groups or whole group discussion:

11	'At the school football match there was…'
12	'There was an ugly riot about…'
13	'We saw a disturbance…'
14	'At the royal wedding…'
15	'This was the rock concert that would…'
16	'This birthday party would be…'
17	'At the meeting to talk about…'

As with the 'Where?' starters, try adding another word or two to give more information about the event:

11a 'At the five-a-side school football match…'

12a 'There was an ugly and violent riot about…'

13a 'We saw an unusual disturbance…'

14a 'At the lavish royal wedding…'

15a 'This was the enormous rock concert that would…'

16a 'This little birthday party would be…'

17a 'At the Town Hall meeting to talk about…'

Starting with Events: What Happened?

A place, 'Where?', and an event, 'What?', can be put together to form a more exciting story starter. Remember that you can adapt the language or style of the story starters to suit particular age and ability groups.

18 'In a faraway land there were celebrations for…'

19 'In the High Street there was a protest about…'

20 'People were gathering in the market square to…'

21 'In a certain house, in a certain street, there was a party that…'

22 'There was something magical happening in the secret garden…'

23 'There was a competition at the swimming pool for…'

24 'There was a meeting of all the members of the after-school club to decide…'

Ideas for Discussion 3

- *Why are some events photographed and others not?*
- *For example, it is usual to take wedding photographs but has anyone seen a funeral photograph? Why not?*
- *Has anyone in the group attended any of the events discussed in the local paper?*
- *Can anyone think of an event they would like to have attended?*
- *Think of an event from the past, or even the future, that you wish you could attend.*

3 Starting with Character: 'Who?'

Start with a group discussion about people we may see in the street or on the train or bus. What do we notice about the way people look, or move, or speak? Do we divide people into those who are like us and those who are different from us? What sort of characters do we enjoy hearing about in stories? For some people it is characters of the same age as themselves, for others it could be heroes or aliens. Encourage observations of how characters walk, the expressions on their faces, what they could be carrying.

The following are a few people starters from contrasting books:

> 'The war ended, and the young men came home, and tried indignantly to fit themselves into old clothes and old habits which proved, on examination, to be both a little threadbare and on trial to be both cripplingly small for bodies and minds mysteriously grown in absence.
>
> *Fallen into the Pit* by Ellis Peters

> 'Two boys stood in the Prince Consort Gallery, and looked down on a third.'
>
> *The Children's Book* by A.S. Byatt

> 'A young man from a small provincial town – a man without independent wealth, without powerful family connections, and without a university education - moved to London in the late 1580s…'
>
> *Will in the World* by Stephen Greenblatt

Starting with Character: Who?

Preliminary Work

We have explored simple ideas for starting stories in particular spaces and places, and then progressed to the idea of different events that happen in these spaces. The next step is to discuss who we are talking about in our stories. Who are the important characters? Are they human or extra-terrestrial? Animals or monsters? Pictures and photographs are ideal for prompting ideas and discussion of characters. Car boot sales are great places to find old family photo albums or try charity shops for old magazines.

* *A holiday poster showing people in another country.*

* *Old family photos, your own or of unknown people.*

* *Postcards of people in different ethnic costume.*

* *Find a book cover that shows an interesting person.*

* *Newspaper photos of a local event involving a famous person.*

* *Charity photos of a child in need.*

* *A clown or similar character in a memorable costume.*

Project Idea

Start a folder with lots of pictures of different people. Encourage the class to bring in pictures of their family (with permission), e.g. photographs from old albums such as family weddings, holiday snaps and naming ceremonies. Try to aim for photographs and postcards of unknown people rather than too many famous people from magazines.

Ideas for Discussion 1

✻ *What is more noticeable, a person's face or what they are wearing?*

✻ *Who impresses us and why?*

✻ *What sort of people influence the way we live or dress?*

✻ *What sort of pictures touch our emotions so that we want to help people?*

✻ *Do film posters make you want to know more about what happens?*

✻ *Find an example of someone who looks kind.*

✻ *Find an example of someone who seems scary.*

Homework Suggestions

b) *Find a postcard showing a person – why do you think they were chosen for this picture?*

c) *Bring in a picture of yourself when you were a baby. Compare this with other people's baby photographs, can you recognise each other? Do people's features or expressions change over time, or remain the same?*

d) *Cut a picture of a pop-star or sports person from a magazine. What made you notice this person?*

e) *Watch a news programme on TV and think about which people you find most interesting.*

f) *Find a photograph or a postcard of a very old person. How do you know that they are old?*

g) *When you are in the street or in a shop, who are the people that you notice?*

h) *When you are out, what sort of people do you avoid?*

Ideas for Discussion 2

- *How do you know if you can trust someone?*
- *What sort of person would you trust to do what they say they will?*
- *In your family, is everyone very different in looks and personality or are there a lot of similarities?*
- *Which of your relatives are you most like?*

Story Starters

The following story starters begin to introduce the idea of characters in stories. Encourage the group to make specific statements about characters rather than generalised ones, and suggest that they use as much detail as possible. Emphasise how interesting characters can bring a story to life.

25 'He was wearing a hooded top, his head bent down, he was hurrying …'

26 'Everyone said how pretty she looked in her party dress but she was feeling…'

27 'The Old Woman paused in the street, she was feeling breathless…'

28 'Fred didn't need be told twice, he jumped on his bike and…'

29 'The man and woman looked as if they were having an argument and they…'

30 'There was a tramp in the park and he…'

31 'Their clothes were bright and cheerful and they were on their way to…'

32 "Grandma – you really shouldn't be here …"

33 'The baby looked healthy and well dressed, gurgling away in the pram, but there was no adult in sight …'

34 "For goodness sake!" she screamed. "You are old enough to know better …"

35 "You are a mean, selfish and cruel person, how could you do that?"

36 'The woman looked enormous, but as she came closer, they could see her enormous billowing cloak…'

37 'The conductor was tall and fair-haired, and looked very elegant in his tail-coat …'

38 'Gary felt fed-up, he just couldn't concentrate. He looked away and saw …'

By adding words describing emotions to the outlines of the characters, as with the examples of the little girl above, we can create different impressions of the character and how they may be feeling. The following are some examples:

25a 'He was wearing a hooded top, his head bent down angrily, he was hurrying…'

26a 'Everyone said how pretty she looked in her party dress but she was feeling scared because…'

27a 'The Old Woman paused in the street, triumphant, even though she was feeling breathless…'

28a 'Fred didn't need to be told twice, zombie-like he jumped on his bike and…'

29a 'The tense man and woman looked as if they were having an argument and they…'

30a 'There was a sad old tramp in the park and he…'

31a 'Their clothes were bright and cheerful, and laughing, they were on their way to…'

Ideas for Discussion 3

✱ *Encourage the group to offer different ideas for expanding the story starters and to illustrate where possible with an example of an extended sentence.*

The following examples are based on the starter line about the little girl in her party dress.

'Everyone said how pretty she looked in her party dress but she was feeling…'

✱ '… **sad** because her friend wasn't at the party, or perhaps because her pet had just died'.
✱ '… **angry** because she hated the colour pink, or because it had belonged to someone else, or because it was scratchy round the arms'.
✱ '… **scared** because she didn't know anyone, or no-one had told her where the toilet was, or she was allergic to something and perhaps people wouldn't understand'.

✱ *Now the emotions have been added to the story starters how does this affect your sentence completion?*

✱ *Look again at story starters 25-38 and see how you could change your story.*

✱ *Look again at some of the pictures of people that the group has collected. What can you tell about how the people are feeling?*

These extended story starters introduce the idea of characters within a context and can be used both as ideas for sentence completion and also for further elaboration. It is useful to introduce the idea of feelings and emotions in relation to the characters and then link these emotions to an event.

In developing the group's StoryBuilding skills we have created ideas about the places for stories, the events that happen in them and people and their emotions who might feature in the stories. Already we have a basic story framework: Where, What and Who?

The ideas in these first three sections can be repeated using different story starters until you feel that the group is ready to move on to new concepts. You could also consider adding illustrations to stories once the ideas have been shared. Ask the group to draw or cut out pictures that they feel are relevant to the story being told.

4 Starting with 'What Else?'

So far, we have had fun with the concepts of place, events and characters in the story, and your group may now be ready to try putting a whole story together, but take care not to get too complicated too quickly.

Developing Characters
Preliminary Work

At this point you can start to discuss ideas for introducing more information into the story. The 'What else?' of the story creates the atmosphere and sets the scene. How do we know the old lady is strong and determined or why Fred is scared of confrontation? Which words or phrases can be used to create the atmosphere, say more about the characters and to add any props that the characters might be carrying or wearing.

The Story of the Old Woman

Following are some questions you could use to explore details of the story and some ideas for additional materials that might help discussion.

Starting with 'What Else?'

'The Old Woman paused in the street, she was feeling breathless…'

* Is the atmosphere in the story going to be scary, friendly or slightly odd?

* We know from the story starter that the woman was old and she was breathless. How old is old? And how can we tell?

* Find some pictures from organisations such as Age Concern that show different types of old people (to prevent stereotypes) and use these for ideas and discussion.

* There are many pictures in Saga magazines and advertisements that show very different types of elderly people. Do these challenge our ideas about age?

* Can the group agree on an image that might be the Old Woman in the story?

* Why do people worry about wrinkles and lines? Illustrate answers with advertisements.

* Share granny stories from popular fairy tales or myths.

Project Idea

Explore more ideas for the Old Woman using images from the group's picture folders, in order to build the character in more detail. You may find that there is very little in the people folder about old people, why might this be?

Ideas for Discussion 1

- *What might the Old Woman be wearing?*

- *Do her clothes make us think she is old?*

- *Is she wearing clothes to look smart, or perhaps clothes to keep warm, or are they the only clothes she has because she is very poor?*

- *Why is she breathless?*

- *Has she walked too far and maybe walked uphill?*

- *Does she have asthma (or another illness) which makes her short of breath?*

- *What other reason might there be for getting breathless?*

These ideas could then lead us to more extended story starters, for example:

'The Old Woman, wearing grubby old clothes, paused in the street. She was breathless and wheezing…'

'The Old Woman paused in the street in the middle of her brisk walk. She was breathless already but determined to press on…'

These two examples give very different impressions of an Old Woman, and open up the possibilities for further observations by the group on different characters and our expectations of them.

Homework Suggestions

a) Discuss with a grandparent or another elderly person the things that are important to them.

b) Ask them how life has changed since they were your age.

c) If possible, ask if you can look at their family photographs.

d) Look for advertisements for products related to getting old.

e) Who are the old people in your favourite TV programmes?

f) Ask friends and family at what point do they think people are 'old'?

g) Find pictures in magazines and newspapers of old people who are in the news.

Ideas for Discussion 2

- Share the information that people have found out about their elderly family members or friends.

- Does this information give us a different perspective on our stories?

- Does anyone have a story to share about an older person that surprised them?

The Story of Fred

'Fred didn't need be told twice, he jumped on his bike and…'

The opening line of the story about Fred is very different because we have so little information except that he has a bicycle and he seems young enough to jump on it. We have no information about of the location of this event. He seems to be old enough to be cycling on his own, but this could cover a wide age range, depending how independent he is. Following are some suggestions to help explore the story and some ideas for additional visual stimulus.

* *Pictures will encourage discussion about different types of bicycles.*

* *Other pictures might show safety helmets, is Fred wearing one?*

* *Create a collage of pictures of boys aged from 7 to 15 and look at differences in physical appearances.*

* *Collect pictures of contrasting boy's clothes and use them for discussion.*

* *Has anyone seen the film 'Home Alone'?*

* *Using a book about boys and emotion, such as* Smasher *(Sunderland, 2008) discuss how Fred might be feeling.*

* *What are the most common feelings for boys to show or to hide?*

Ideas for Discussion 2

✻ *Share the information that people have found out about their elderly family members or friends.*

✻ *Does this information give us a different perspective on our stories?*

✻ *Does anyone have a story to share about an older person that surprised them?*

The Story of Fred

'Fred didn't need be told twice, he jumped on his bike and…'

The opening line of the story about Fred is very different because we have so little information except that he has a bicycle and he seems young enough to jump on it. We have no information about of the location of this event. He seems to be old enough to be cycling on his own, but this could cover a wide age range, depending how independent he is. Following are some suggestions to help explore the story and some ideas for additional visual stimulus.

* *Pictures will encourage discussion about different types of bicycles.*

* *Other pictures might show safety helmets, is Fred wearing one?*

* *Create a collage of pictures of boys aged from 7 to 15 and look at differences in physical appearances.*

* *Collect pictures of contrasting boy's clothes and use them for discussion.*

* *Has anyone seen the film 'Home Alone'?*

* *Using a book about boys and emotion, such as* Smasher *(Sunderland, 2008) discuss how Fred might be feeling.*

* *What are the most common feelings for boys to show or to hide?*

Project Idea

Ask the group to check the folders to see if there is any useful information for the story about Fred. Encourage them to find more material relevant to Fred's story to add to the three folders 'Where?', 'What?' and 'Who?'.

Starting with 'What Else?'

Ideas for Discussion 3

❋ *Who do we think Fred is?*

❋ *How old is he and what clothes is he wearing?*

❋ *Has somebody told him something?*

❋ *What could this be?*

❋ *Does anyone know where he is?*

❋ *Is he usually out on his bicycle on his own?*

❋ *Has being alone made him scared, excited or worried?*

The following are two contrasting examples of extensions of Fred's story starter.

❋ *'Fred didn't need to be told twice when his mother approached him, he jumped on his bike and rode quickly to his sister's school…''Fred didn't need to be told twice when the masked man shouted at him to make himself scarce; he jumped on his bike, his heart beating with fear and rode off as quickly as he could…'*

Homework Suggestions

a) *Find a photograph of yourself when you were three years younger than now or of someone else at that age. What is different?*

b) *Look at different magazines written for boys and think about which one you can relate to the best.*

c) *Try on a mask or even a pair of goggles and see how different you look.*

d) *Look for different pictures of boys with bicycles, and try to find one who fits your idea of Fred.*

e) *Who is your favourite boy character on television and why?*

f) *Do you have a cousin or older brother that you respect?*

g) *Which boy characters in stories and films do you admire?*

Ideas for Discussion 4

❋ *Encourage the group to explore more about the character they have created for Fred.*

❋ *Is he someone they would relate to?*

❋ *What does he need to do in order to be respected?*

❋ *Do they think he has a brother, if so, is he older or younger than Fred?*

❋ *Is Fred scared about what is happening, or does he feel brave?*

Developing the Atmosphere

Preliminary Work

The step to creating an atmosphere of the story is a big one, as it has more to do with impressions than concrete events. Did it feel scary and chilly? Or warm and friendly? What do we *sense* is going on? Once the group can recognise how to create an atmosphere, their StoryBuilding will enter new dimensions of imagination. Everyone has experienced atmospheres that feel excited or friendly or even hostile, or have been aware of tensions that they cannot explain. Find additional stimuli that can help the group to understand the concept of building an atmosphere for their stories.

* *Find a poster that illustrates an atmospheric scene, maybe for a film or play.*

* *Play a CD of sound effects such as thunder or relaxation music, to create general feelings.*

* *Play a CD with sound effects of specific events, such as cars screeching to a halt or trains moving. What sort of atmosphere can sounds create?*

* *As a group, think of words that create different atmospheres such as: spooky, scary, odd, still, excited.*

* *Which words would the group use to describe the impressions given by CDs or the poster?*

* *Use small percussion instruments such as wood blocks or bells to create sound effects to accompany sentences or story starters.*

Project Idea

Start to create a fourth folder using atmospheric pictures that the group might find in magazines or written descriptions from films, books or plays.

Ideas for Discussion 1

An open group discussion is a useful forum for everyone to share something about atmospheres. Be aware that you may well get some personal disclosures here if children have difficulties at home: there maybe a threat of violence or a feeling of tension about the family breaking up. This is not the time for personal issues to be explored and people can be encouraged to describe the atmospheres in their stories. In this way, their experiences can be acknowledged without taking them further. If levels of distress or worry are revealed that you feel give cause for concern, show that you have appreciated these feelings and then follow up after the session if you feel it appropriate.

✱ *Can anyone think of an atmosphere that was tense or cool or welcoming or unfriendly?*

✱ *Has anyone felt disgust, horror, sick or revolted by an atmosphere rather than directly by an image?*

- *Was there a feeling of violence in the air?*

- *What sort of atmosphere can be created by unexplained noises such as drips, tapping, footsteps or creaks and groans?*

- *Can anyone describe an atmosphere that they felt but could not explain.*

- *Has anyone experienced an atmosphere that someone else explained away with what they knew was not a truthful explanation.*

- *Do different people experience atmospheres in a different ways?*

Homework Suggestions

a) *Suggest that group members watch a television show or play where the director has tried to create an atmosphere – was it believable?*

b) *Did the atmosphere tell you more about the story or did it all feel a bit stupid?*

c) *Try moving through different spaces: the classroom, gym, garden, chapel or church, concert space; how does the atmosphere change?*

d) *Listen for sounds in the countryside or street or market that create an atmosphere.*

e) *Observe whether it is sounds or pictures that create the strongest atmosphere.*

f) *Notice how people react to certain sounds: a siren, a scream, the screech of brakes, does everyone do so in the same way?*

g) *Record some sounds and use them to create a background for a story.*

Story Starters

Explore the following story starters and encourage sentence completion, focussing on the atmosphere being created.

38 'Crisp snow crunched underfoot when…'

39 'Suddenly the moon skipped behind the clouds and…'

40 'There was a bark of a fox and a howl of a lone wolf and…'

41 'The door creaked, that was the only sound as…'

42 'A screech of brakes, a sickening thud and…'

43 'Just a baby crying, crying without stopping and…'

44 'Was it thunder or an explosion from the quarry? Or maybe something more sinister?'

Using the story starters about the Old Woman and Fred we are already establishing some atmosphere by developing their characters and the location of the story. Try to expand this further by developing the atmosphere.

'The Old Woman paused in the empty, cobbled street, in the middle of her brisk walk. She was breathless but keen to press on, especially as something was making her feel uneasy...'

'It was getting dark on this damp autumn evening. At the end of the lane near the woods Fred sensed that he was not alone. He didn't need to be told twice when suddenly a masked man shouted at him to make himself scarce. He jumped on his bike, his heart beating with fear and rode off as quickly as he could...'

Ideas for Discussion 2

We have introduced the idea of *uneasiness* with the old lady, that something is not quite right. This gives something else for the group to explore and the chance to examine their own feelings of unease and the importance of trusting these (think about and compare other words such as disease, ease).

In Fred's story, he *senses* something, and then suddenly something happens. It is important that children and young people are able to make use of their own senses, perhaps by first giving senses some reality in a story. We have already explored the visual and audio senses above; what about taste, smell and touch?

Project Idea – Sense Stimulus

In order to encourage a full range of sensory responses, bring in different things for the group to touch, smell and taste to encourage greater sensory experience: e.g. fresh apples, cuddly puppet, lemons, fresh herbs, lavender, velvet cushion, sandpaper, shaving foam. Sensory stimulus encourages the development of associations such as, 'This sandpaper feels rough, just like …'. (When using food, be alert to possible allergies and only use non-perfumed shaving foam.)

Developing the Props

Preliminary Work

Props are objects that the characters carry or wear or interact with in order to tell us more about who they are and what they do. So Harry Potter's wand or Gandalf's stick or a scientist's equipment are all important props that add to stories.

Props that do more than expected are a very effective storytelling device, so when the broomsticks start multiplying in 'The Sorcerer's Apprentice' it raises the tension of the story. Many events that occur in stories (and in our everyday lives) have lots of props that accompany them: for example a wedding involves rings, flowers, photographs and documents. A long-distance lorry driver needs maps, navigation tools, HGV driving licence, sleeping equipment (if he sleeps in the cab), break-down resources.

Starting with 'What Else?'

Ideas for Discussion

Ask the group to bring in some props or pictures of props, such as:

* *Mobile phone (use a discarded or toy phone)*

* *A large wooden spoon*

* *A large key*

* *A chef's hat or a policeman's helmet*

* *Dark glasses*

* *Feather duster*

* *Lace veil*

Encourage the group to think about and discuss the props they have collected. Explore who would wear or carry these items and what more they might add to a character in the story.

Story Starters

45 'The amazing hat was the first thing you'd notice when…'

46 'Cap in hand he went…'

47 'Not an ordinary stick, but one with a brass head in the shape of a lion…'

48 'The helmet, the handcuffs, now he knew…'

49 'Black boots, polished and shiny; boots with spurs were…'

50 'Wooden clogs on her feet, wooden stick in her hand, she…'

51 'He tapped his cane impatiently and again…'

Starting with 'What Else?'

Starting with 'What Else?'

52 'He carried a wooden box with great care, it was made of rosewood…'

53 'Balancing an enormous three-tier cake, the chef walked…'

54 '"The letter is here, at last," she called out…'

55 'The parcel looked untidy, with torn brown paper, and loose string…'

Now we can explore what will happen when we add props to our ongoing stories about the Old Woman and Fred, bearing in mind that Fred already has a bicycle and the new character in his story is wearing a mask.

The Old Woman paused in the empty, cobbled street, in the middle of her brisk walk. She felt a little warm and loosened her scarf, hitching up her bag at the same time. She leaned on her walking stick as she was breathless, but she was determined to press on, especially as something was making her feel uneasy. Her stout stick gave her some comfort…

It was getting dark on this damp autumn evening. At the end of the lane near the woods Fred re-packed his rucksack. He sensed that he was not alone. He didn't need to be told twice when suddenly a masked man, waving a claw hammer, shouted at him to make himself scarce. He jumped on his bike, his heart beating with fear and rode off as quickly as he could…

Developing Places & Spaces

Preliminary Work

The place of the story can also be developed with more information, and the idea of different spaces can be introduced. Initially we could add descriptions of the place by using more adjectives such as 'dark', 'grey', 'deserted', 'bright', 'friendly'. Try to find pictures with obvious place and space elements to use for stimulus.

Ideas for Discussion 1

* *Decide whether the story is taking place in an urban environment, in the town or the city, or is it located in the countryside?*

* *Use natural environments, is the story taking place at sea or in the desert or the jungle or in the middle of nowhere?*

* *Is it pouring with rain or brilliant sunshine or cold and bleak?*

* *Do thunder storms, lightning or rainbows feature in the tale?*

* *Does this story happen indoors or outdoors, or does it move between several spaces?*

* *Consider whether the story is happening in this world or outer space, in another consciousness or parallel universe?*

* *Do events take place underground or in a cave or inside an old barn?*

By introducing the idea of space and not just place the group's StoryBuilding, skills can be developed. Encourage discussion about 'place and space', are these different ideas and in what way? Create a list of as many different space words as the group can come up with.

- *Is it a public space or a private space or a personal space?*
- *Is the space empty or perhaps crowded?*
- *Is the space cramped or vast?*
- *Are people banned from entering this space?*
- *Is it a suffocating space?*
- *What feelings does the space provoke? Do characters feel breathless, overwhelmed or claustrophobic?*
- *Is it a space that you would miss and want to visit again?*

Story Starters

56 'The sun rose over the dark mountains, a red glow welcomed in the day of…'

57 'The strong iron doors looked forbidding, a car drew up and…'

58 'The curtains were drawn in the little house so…'

59 'Where is this place with its high walls and tall trees?'

60 'What is this place with its high walls and no trees?'

61 'The river splashed over the stones, the water buttercups glowed bright yellow, and a woodpecker tapped in the nearby woods. Then…'

62 'Crumbling rocks, and a tumbledown barn, gave an atmosphere of neglect. So…'

We can now develop more ideas of place and space for the Old Woman and Fred and the context of their stories:

> *The Old Woman stopped suddenly, in the distance she could hear a rumble of thunder, and the drizzle started to make spots on the cobbles. She remembered that she had left her umbrella at home, in the stand in the hallway. Could she make her destination without getting soaking wet? She turned up her collar and set off again, taking care on the wet stones …*

> *Fred realised he had fallen asleep under the tree and it was getting dark; he could hardly see the edges of the wood and the smell told him there was a fire somewhere …*

5   Starting with Time: 'When?'

We can now include concepts of time in the stories of Fred and the Old Woman and we can see that by varying the ideas, we can create a very different situation. We can use the idea of waiting to increase the tension in the story or to do the exact opposite by being casual about the time. Do we know the time because of a clock striking? Or the position of the sun? Or we have glanced at our watches?

> *Although the Old Woman worried that she might be late, she paused in the empty, cobbled street, in the middle of her brisk walk. She felt a little warm and loosened her scarf, hitching up her bag at the same time. The clock struck the hour, she might be late. She leaned on her walking stick as she was breathless but she was determined to press on, especially as something was making her feel uneasy. Her heavy watch was reminding her of the time. Her stout stick gave her some comfort...*

> *Slowly the moon went behind the clouds, it was almost night time. It was getting dark on this damp autumn evening. At the end of the lane near the woods Fred took his time as he re-packed his rucksack. He sensed that he was not alone. He didn't need to be told twice when suddenly a masked man, waving a claw hammer, shouted at him to make himself scarce. Immediately he jumped on his bike, his heart beating with fear and rode off as quickly as he could...*

So far we have examined several starting points for stories: locations, events, characters, atmospheres, props, and elaborated characters and spaces. Many ideas for group discussion and homework have also been explored. The stories of the Old Woman and Fred have been elaborated in different ways and we have seen how contexts and perspectives can change significantly with the use of different atmospheres and descriptive words.

The next big step in developing storytelling is introducing the concept of time frames. For many children, the concept of time is difficult and we will consider how to develop time in order to have clarity and staged learning. As mentioned above in the discussion of child development, children begin to develop the idea of time from about three years of age, but we need to introduce the concepts in gradual stages.

Preliminary Work

Developmentally, we know that children and young people, especially those with special learning needs, can have difficulty with concepts of time. There are also many variations cross-culturally in time concepts and many western words do not translate into other languages. The English language has some very specific time-related and words and phrases such as 'now', 'later', or 'in ten minutes time' or 'next week'. In other countries attitudes and references to time are less specific, a joke in Greece is: 'Do you mean an English ten minutes?' (meaning exactly 10 minutes), or 'Do you mean a Greek ten minutes?' (meaning anything up to 25 minutes!).

You may need to adapt the language you use, depending on the age of your group. The story starters on the following pages can be worked on within the group in discussion, and several phrases can be compared.

Project Idea

Start a folder that contains ideas for timed events: encourage the group to bring in pictures or descriptions of events from local newspapers or other sources that can include everything from weddings to sports events, including festivals of drama or music, natural events such as an eclipse or solstice, even meetings of clubs and societies, and so on.

Starting with Time: When?

The following opening lines from books all use time to introduce the story.

> 'Mariam was five years old the first time she heard the word *harami*.
> It happened on a Thursday.'
> *A Thousand Splendid Suns* by Khaled Hosseini

> 'At seven o'clock on the morning that he was killed Abed Takkoush parked his Mercedes outside the Ribiera hotel…'
> *War Stories* by Jeremy Bowen

Brian Keenan's account of his kidnapping in Beirut starts in an interesting fashion:

> 'It is always difficult to find a beginning. All good stories have one, no matter how inconclusive or unexpected their end may be. The end of this story has not yet come, so it is particularly difficult to know where to begin.'
> *An Evil Cradling* by Brian Keenan

Think of all the ways in which people can begin a story, the most well known is 'Once upon a time…' There are others such as: 'A long time ago…', 'Now, in the time of…', 'You will never guess what happened yesterday…'

We can see immediately from these examples that many stories start with time. Perhaps one of the most famous story starters is 'It was the best of times, it was the worst of times' (*A Tale of Two Cities,* Charles Dickens). Immediately, this engages our attention and we want to know what comes next.

Ideas for Discussion 1

✹ *Give examples of familiar stories that start with the idea of time, especially for groups who are lacking in confidence.*

✹ *Dr Who or other space travel stories are good sources of stories that move forwards and backwards in time.*

✹ *Create a story based on any of the story starters to illustrate how we 'build a story'.*

✹ *Within the group, discuss different time starters, to help, you could prepare some opening lines from age-appropriate stories. These could be taken from books, magazines or newspapers. Glue them on to pieces of card and pass them round the group; group members may recognise them. Use these as a basis for discussion.*

Homework Suggestions

a) *Find different pictures of clocks and compare their uses within the group.*

b) *Think about what time certain events happen at home. What happens at school, is there is a difference?*

c) *Can you remember what happened on holiday last summer?*

d) *Note the time when your favourite television programme starts and ends.*

e) *Look in local and national newspapers for the day and time, and duration of special events.*

f) *Next week there is something special happening, what could it be?*

Story Starters

There are various activities you can use to introduce the idea of time: 'What time do we start school?' (show the time on the clock) 'What time is play time?' and so on. The following are simple time-based story starters for the group to discuss and complete.

63 'A long time ago there lived…"

64 'This morning John went…'

65 'At 9 o'clock the school door opens so…'

66 'The clock struck six so we knew the fish and chip shop was open…'

67 'Every day she felt unhappy because…'

68 'Tomorrow something special will happen…'

69 'Today, Mary was feeling very happy because…'

Starting with Time: When?

Starting with Time: When?

70 'Not now Charlie, please wait until later…'

71 'You wait until Saturday – she will find out then…'

72 'At some time in the future you will have to make a decision…'

73 'It was the longest ten minutes I have ever waited…'

74 'He pressed the stop-watch, "Now!", he shouted…'

75 'Millions of years old, he thought, looking at the fossil…'

Ideas for Discussion 2

✻ Ask the group to share their own experiences and feelings about time. Discuss who is relaxed about time, who always wants something to happen right now, and who gets frustrated when others expect something immediately.

✻ How do the group deal with the school timetable?

✻ What time-based routines do you have at home?

✻ Are these different at weekends?

✻ Are there variations between different cultural groups?

✻ Does your approach to time depend on how old you are?

Story Starters

76	'After the rain stops she will…'
77	'Today we had my favourite lesson which was…'
78	'Before she could shout, he…'
79	'Not long ago there was…'
80	'Soon we will be able to…'
81	'"Not now!", shouted her mum. She was…'
82	'When the exams are over we can…'

Continue with the following story starters if the group is ready; you will find that some group members complete the starters with factual statement, others will create an imaginary event. There is no right or wrong way to respond.

Story Starters

83	'It was announced today that…'
84	'In future, everyone will be expected to…'
85	'Yesterday, I had a terrible shock…'
86	'In ancient times there were…'
87	'I had a phone call this morning that…'
88	'At four o'clock you will stay behind and…'
89	'The clock struck seven, was it morning or evening?…'

Starting with Time: When?

Encourage group members to come up with their own ideas for time-related starters and write them on the board. You could also work together with the same story starter and ask the group questions in order to elaborate a story as in the following examples.

90 'At nine o'clock this morning…'
Did you see something? Meet someone? Feel something? Remember something? Have a strange sensation?

91 'Long ago and far away…'
Who lived then? Where did they live? Were they famous? Were they in danger? What happened?

92 'At sunrise…'
What colour was the sky? Was anyone there? What was the atmosphere? Did something happen?

93 'It was the middle of winter…'
Was there snow? What was the temperature? What were you doing? Who else was there? What country was this in?

Ideas for Discussion 3

✻ *Discuss the differences between phrases relating to time in different ways, precise references e.g. 9 o'clock, more general, e.g. next Tuesday and very general e.g. last year.*

✻ *Think of ideas of each type of reference to time in stories.*

✻ *When would time need to be precise in a story and when could it be vague, or just a general indication?*

Developing the Concept of Time

As well as developing the places, events and characters in the story with more information, we can also include more detail about the time. As we have seen, time can be located in the past, present or future and be approximate or exact. People have different ideas about concepts of time, for instance one person's definition of 'soon' could be 'almost immediately', while another's might be 'in a few days'.

Starting with Time: When?

Ideas for Discussion

* Think of different ways to elaborate the time frame in a story. For example, what was the exact time that the announcement was made, how far in the future is the expected change, or at what time yesterday did the shock occur?

* The seasons can also contribute to the description of a time frame. Is it spring, summer, autumn or winter? Does the seasonal weather make a difference to the story?

* Does it matter if the event happened in the morning, at midday, in the afternoon, evening or at night? Perhaps it happened at dawn or dusk? At sunrise or sundown?

* This could lead on to ideas of whether there was a clock striking or whether the person had a watch, or if the sun was high overhead.

6 Developing the Plot & Story Endings

We have stayed with the Old Woman and Fred and elaborated their starting points by introducing the concept of time. Various different types of story starter have been applied to their stories. The two stories that have been started and developed using the StoryBuilding approach can now be finished.

We have the beginnings of the two contrasting short stories that have been built in clearly defined stages. We now need to consider where these stories will go in relation to their plot – what actually happens?

In this final chapter, plot development and different ways to end a story will be explored. The stories of the Old Woman and Fred will finally have 'a beginning, middle and end'. By working through a complete story, groups will begin to understand the structure of stories.

Some people do not like stories that appear incomplete, or that 'leave them hanging'. A small child responds to stories because of the structure, and young people and adults with special needs can get quite anxious if they do not discover the ending of a story.

Developing the Plot & Story Endings

> A young man of 20 years old followed me around in one workshop and kept tugging at my sleeve, 'Did Mihai escape from the wolf or did it eat him?' And then later, he asked me again, 'What really happened in the story, I want to know'. He was only satisfied when in small groups they made up their own ending and he was able to choose the one he liked best: one where Mihai was not eaten up by the wolf!

This section will look at what happens after the story starts, how can we help the story to develop? Once we have our extended story starter, then the plot will become easier to develop because already we have ideas about place, event, people, atmospheres, props and time. Since the stories of the Old Woman and Fred are getting more complex we can see how they develop further. Essentially we are looking at 'what happens next?' which is the 'How?' of the story progressing.

Ideas for Discussion

* What sort of stories or soaps do the group find interesting because of what happens?

* Discuss examples of stories that hold people's attention or which had unexpected plots.

* Do people have a preference for realistic stories such as those about people who are familiar to us, or do they like to escape with stories about the distant past, or science fiction, or magical realms?

Homework Suggestions

a) *Watch an episode of a police drama and see how the plot unfolds.*

b) *Think of a time when you were surprised at what happened in a story and why you expected it to turn out differently.*

c) *Find pictures in magazines or newspapers that illustrate the plot of a story – perhaps something that has happened locally.*

d) *Find an advertisement for a new film and see if you can tell what the plot is from the picture.*

e) *What sort of a plot would interest your parents?*

f) *What sort of plots appeals more to girls than boys?*

How can we develop the stories of the Old Woman and Fred in order to complete their stories? What is the plot? So far we have elaborated the place, event, characters, atmosphere, props and time. What can be added based on the information we already know?

Ideas for Plot Development

The Story of the Old Woman

1. *Where do you think the Old Woman is going?*

2. *What is she going to do?*

3. *Who is she going to meet?*

4. *When will this take place?*

5. *She is feeling uneasy because she is being followed.*

6. *She is feeling uneasy because she is meeting someone who could be violent.*

7. *She is feeling uneasy because she can sense that something is wrong.*

8. *She knows some information that others want to get hold of.*

9 She is carrying something precious that she needs to hide. What could this be?

10 It is her last opportunity to have a reconciliation with her daughter.

11 It is the only time that she will ever be able to walk on the moors again.

12 She is being pursued because she has stolen something.

13 Police are looking for her because she is a suspect in a murder case.

14 She wants to safeguard some rare bird eggs before they are stolen.

Groups will be surprised at just how many variations there are on a theme that could fit the story starter that we have devised about the Old Woman. Suggest they choose their favourite one and in small groups finish the story. The following example shows one possibility:

The Old Woman paused in the empty, cobbled street, in the middle of her brisk walk. It was early spring and the air was a little chilly. She leaned on her walking stick as she was breathless, but she was determined to press on, especially as something was making her feel uneasy. Her stout stick gave her some comfort and she hurried forwards for her important meeting. Every so often she listened for any sounds that might tell her that the other person had arrived.

She reached the lane past the old barn and beyond it was a small wood; you could not see from the road but there was a small hut in the wood that had once belonged to a charcoal burner. She sat down outside the hut on an old log and waited. She heard him before she could see him but then at last he was there. "Fred," she called out. "You have made it."

Fred got off his bicycle and took off his helmet. He sat down on the ground to catch his breath and gave the Old Woman a grin. She was about to ask a question but he said, "Don't worry, I have it with me" and he took out an envelope that had been hidden in his helmet. The Old Woman looked as if she might cry, but she didn't. She just took the envelope and looked inside. She nodded and said "All is well – thank you, thank you so much."

Fred said, "Can I know what it is, after all the trouble I had in getting it?" "Of course" she said, "but it is a long story…"

Suggest to the class that they work in small groups to tell the next part of the story. Questions that might be useful are:

* *What was in the envelope?*

* *How does the Old Woman know Fred?*

* *Why is it so important?*

* *Is the masked man anything to do with the story?*

Next, the group can use Fred's story starter and continue the story from his point of view. Think about his ride home, how he obtained the envelope and cycled to meet the Old Woman.

> *It was getting dark on this damp autumn evening at the end of the lane near the woods. As Fred re-packed his rucksack, he sensed that he was not alone. He didn't need to be told twice when suddenly a masked man, waving a claw hammer, shouted at him to make himself scarce; he jumped on his bike, his heart beating with fear and rode off home as quickly as he could…*

Ideas for Story Endings

What is the best ending for a story? One that is unexpected? A loving ending? A sad ending? One where justice is done? How would the group like to end the story of the Old Woman and Fred? Discuss some of the following and add more ideas from the group:

1. *After Fred was sent to prison the Old Woman visited him, she felt she was to blame for asking him to steal the document.*

2. *When the Old Woman was sent to prison, Fred visited her and he kept her secret safe. It would only be a few months and then they could prove what really happened.*

3. *Inside the envelope was a PIN number that would allow the woman to access the money that had been stolen by her lodger. Now she could rest at ease, and Fred would visit her for company.*

4. *The Old Woman now had the map that would show where the family jewels had been hidden.*

5 *Fred found he could really talk to the Old Woman and explain all his troubles at home; she was a good listener.*

6 *Fred agreed to take the next step and find the Old Woman's missing manuscript.*

7 *DNA tests - that was what it had all been about. Fred's mother turns out to be the Old Woman's daughter who was adopted. But that is another story…*

Now the group have decided for themselves how they story will end. They have learned how to create their own story through StoryBuilding using the '4 W's + H' in a variety of settings, as well as following the approach through to create a complete narrative. All of these ideas can be used in a variety of ways and mixed together in different formats.

Time for a new story!

Section Two

Resources & Bibliography

Name: _____   Date: _____

1 Where is this tree growing – describe the place and what else might be there?
   _____

2 Who planted the tree and do they still care for it?
   _____

3 When was the tree planted?
   _____

4 What sort of stories could someone tell about this tree?
   _____

5 Why has the tree survived for so long, and is it a strong tree?
   _____

Put all these answers together and you have a story about the tree.

 This page may be photocopied for instructional use only. © *StoryBuilding*, S. Jennings, 2010

Name: _____   Date: _____

1. Colour the balloons and the girl while you think about stories.
   _____

2. Choose one of the balloon words to decide how you will start your story, e.g. if it is 'Who?', describe someone who will be a character in your story.
   _____

3. Start to build your story by taking one word at a time from the balloons and adding it to your story.
   _____

4. Make sure that your story has an ending and that you have described 'what happened' in the story.
   _____

5. Draw your own picture to illustrate your story.
   _____

Name: _____ Date: _____

This announcement appeared in the grocery store, the post-office and outside the church.

1 Who do you think the cat belongs to?
_____

2 Where might it have gone?
_____

3 When could it have happened?
_____

4 What should the owner do now?
_____

5 Create an ending for the story. Decide whether the cat was taken or whether it got lost.
_____

Daily ✠ Bugle

Saturday 9 October 2010   80p

Contact! Escape shaft reaches Chilean miners trapped underground for 65 days!

Name: _____   Date: _____

1   What must it feel like to be trapped underground for so long?
    _____

2   How do the men keep themselves cheerful?
    _____

3   What do you think that they miss most?
    _____

4   What would you miss if you were trapped for somewhere for a long time?
    _____

5   What sort of stories will the miners tell their families when they get home?
    _____

6   Think of a story that one miner might tell: include a description of where he was, how he was feeling and how it felt to be free again.
    _____

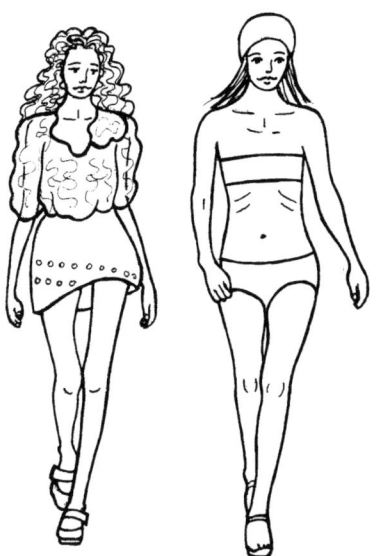

Name: _____ Date: _____

1 Why do you think models are so thin? Do they have a choice?
_____

2 Why is there so much pressure for girls to be thin even though many magazine pictures have been changed with an airbrush?
_____

3 How could we change people's ideas about the difference between slimness and thinness?
_____

4 What might a very thin person be feeling inside?
_____

5 Think of a story about a girl who would like to be a model and tries to make herself thin. What might make her decide to do this and how does she feel inside?
_____

 This page may be photocopied for instructional use only. © *StoryBuilding*, S. Jennings, 2010

Name: _____   Date: _____

The old lady lives on her own in a house at the edge of the woods. One day she is visited by a young deaf girl called Sarah Moon, and they gradually get to know each other.

1 Describe the house where the Old Woman lives.
_____

2 Why do you think she lives on her own?
_____

3 Is she pleased to meet the young girl?
_____

4 Where has Sarah Moon come from?
_____

5 Write a story about how the girl and the Old Woman befriend each other.
_____

References

Boston L.M., 1992, *Memories,* Oldknow Books, Huntingdon

Bowen J., 2006, *War Stories*, Simon & Schuster, London

Byatt A.S., 2009/2010, *The Children's Book*, Vintage, London

Cameron J., 1974/1986, *An Indian Summer*, Penguin, Harmondsworth

Cornwall P., 2007, *Book of the Dead,* Little Brown, London

Crystal B., 2008 *Shakespeare on Toast*, Icon, London

Dickens C., 1984, *A Tale of Two Cities,* Bantam Classics, London

Greenblatt S., 2005, *Will in the World*, Pimlico, London

Hoffman J., 2007, *Plea of Insanity,* Penguin, Harmondsworth

Hosseini K., 2007, *A Thousand Splendid Suns*, Bloomsbury, London

Jennings S., 2004, *Creative Storytelling with Children at Risk,* Speechmark, Milton Keynes

Jennings S., 2006, *Creative Storytelling with Adults at Risk,* Speechmark, Milton Keynes

Keenan B., 1993, *An Evil Cradling,* Vintage, London

Peters E., 1951/1991, *Fallen into the Pit*, Futura Publications, London

Pratchett T., 2000, *The Truth,* Doubleday, London

References

Pullman P., 2007, *His Dark Materials,* Scholastic, New York

Shakespeare W., 2005, *The Winter's Tale,* Penguin Classics, Harmondsworth

Sunderland M., 2007, *Smasher: A story to help adolescents with anger & alienation,* Hinton House Publishers, Buckingham

Van Der Post L., 1961/1965, *The Heart of the Hunter*, Penguin, Harmondsworth

Further Reading

Crimmens P., 2004, *Storymaking and Creative Groupwork with Older People*, Jessica Kingsley, London

Crimmens P., 2006, *Drama Therapy and Storymaking in Special Education*, Jessica Kingsley, London

Gersie A. & King N., 1991, *Storymaking in Education and Therapy*, Jessica Kingsley, London

Vickers S. & Emanuel R., 2011, *The Stories Within: Developing Inclusive Drama & Storymaking*, Hinton House Publishers, Buckingham

The Stories Within

Developing inclusive drama and story-making

Sheree Vickers & Rosie Emanuel

Ages 5 to adult

A comprehensive toolkit for creating inclusive drama & storytelling.

This practical, photocopiable book provides an innovative approach to developing inclusive story-making and drama with both children and adults.

Emphasises developing original stories rather than using traditional storylines or scripts, shows how to create drama games or adapt existing ones to the specific needs of your group.

Includes: Preparation & planning; Creating a sensory storytelling kit; Developing inclusive practice in schools and groups; Working with adults: rediscovering play & creating age-appropriate stories; Practical workshop structures; Problems, strategies & solutions.

Ideal for use by teachers, drama practitioners and therapists this practical handbook provides the tools needed to create original drama and stories. These ideas can be used with individuals and groups with a variety of needs.

2011 ♦ 192pp ♦ A4 paperback ♦ ISBN 978-1-906531-22-5 ♦ £29.99

info@hintonpublishers.com • www.hintonpublishers.com